MW00607506

better together*

*This book is best read together, grownup and kid.

 akidsco.com

a kids book about

a kids book about

INCARCERATION

by Ethan Thrower

a
kids
book
about

Text and design copyright © 2022
by A Kids Book About, Inc.

Copyright is good! It ensures that work like this can exist,
and more work in the future can be created.

All rights reserved. No part of this publication may be
reproduced, distributed, or transmitted in any form or
by any means, including photocopying, recording, other
electronic or mechanical methods, without the prior
written permission of the publisher, except in the case of
brief quotations embodied in critical reviews and certain
other noncommercial uses permitted by copyright law.
For permission requests, write to the publisher.

Printed in the United States of America.

A Kids Book About books are available online: *akidsco.com*

To share your stories, ask questions, or inquire about bulk
purchases (schools, libraries, and nonprofits), please use
the following email address: *hello@akidsco.com*

ISBN: 978-1-953955-58-6

Designed by Rick DeLucco
Edited by Emma Wolf

To Kaiyah and Kaelyn.

And my community who
never stopped believing in me.

Intro

Incarceration is something our children will define for themselves through media, their peers, and stereotypes—unless we talk about it with them first. Stories of incarceration go untold for a range of reasons. This silence can leave our kids uncertain of how to ask questions, share, get help, learn, and cope.

Every experience with incarceration is different, and so are the feelings and opinions involved. Your kid may bring up questions you're not ready to fully answer, or maybe can't answer. And that's OK.

After reading this book, I hope kids understand what incarceration is, what life is like in prison, the power of choices and the impact our choices have on ourselves and others, and that the experiences and emotions that come with knowing someone who is incarcerated are valid.

I imagine bigger conversations will take place around rules, responsibility, social justice, mass incarceration, healing, and change—these are some powerful things to dive into. I invite you to lean into them versus shy away.

Thank you for being a supportive grownup who is willing to open up honest communication about this BIG topic.

My name is Ethan.

I'm a dad,

a husband,

and a school social worker
who talks to kids every day.

When I was in high school,
I got good grades and my
favorite sport was track.

I was *really fast* and won
almost all of my races!

At the end of my my senior year
I didn't walk across the stage
for graduation.

I wasn't at the ceremony because I was

INCARCERATED.

Do you know what incarceration is?

Incarceration is when somebody is sent to jail* or prison after being accused or found guilty of a crime.

*We'll cover some big terms in this book. Each time you see an underlined word (like jail), know you can find out more about it at the end of the book.

Committing a crime is a choice
a lot of people make.

Did you know over 10 million people in the world are incarcerated,[1] and almost 50% of people in the United States are close to someone who is incarcerated?[2]

[1] Roy Walmsley, "World Prison Population List: Eleventh Edition," National Institute of Corrections, January 19, 2021, https://nicic.gov/world-prison-population-listeleventh-edition.

[2] "Half of Americans Have Family Members Who Have Been Incarcerated," Equal Justice Initiative, November 15, 2019, https://eji.org/news/half-of-americans-have-family-members-who-have-been-incarcerated/.

You may be wondering:

Why were you in prison?

Why did you commit a crime?

How long were you there?

What was it like?

Was it safe?

Will you ever have to go back?

There's a lot that's easy to talk about, like what prison looked like, how I kept in touch with my family, and what I ate.

But what incarceration is
and why I was there are much,
much harder to talk about.

So let's talk about that first.

Incarceration is meant to be a consequence* for committing a crime.

*A consequence is the result of a poor decision you make.

Let's look at some of those crimes.

A NOTE: This might bring up some complicated feelings for some of you, especially if you've been impacted by them.

Some choices that are crimes are...

ABUSE:

when someone hurts or causes someone harm. This includes emotional, financial, sexual, physical, and other abuse. This can happen to anyone of any age.

ASSAULT:

physically harming someone.

BURGLARY:

going into a place that doesn't belong to you and taking something that isn't yours.

DRUG DEALING:

selling substances or drugs that aren't legal.

ROBBERY:

taking something that does not belong to you, sometimes while holding a weapon, like a gun.

My crime was armed robbery.
I used a weapon—a gun—to take
money that didn't belong to me.

For committing armed robbery, I was incarcerated and served a mandatory minimum sentence of 8 1/2 years* in prison.

*So if you are 9 right now, that is almost your whole life.

When I was in prison:

My name became a number. People in charge no longer called me Ethan.

I had clothing.

But I was given a uniform.

I wore the same clothes
everyone else wore——blue jeans,
a blue shirt, and tennis shoes.

I got to eat.

But I didn't get to choose
when that was or what I ate.

I talked to my family through letters that were opened and read before I got them, phone calls that were recorded, and visits that were supervised and sometimes behind thick glass.

Being in prison isn't like
anything you could imagine.

It's not like it is in
video games or movies.

It's a really hard place to be.

People spend a lot of time in their prison cells, sometimes 20–23 hours a day.

That is almost the whole day.

A cell is the room you live in
when you're in prison.

It's really small.

I COULD TOUCH THE

MY ARMS WHEN I ST

There are bars instead of a door and walls, and a lock

WALLS WITH BOTH

OOD IN THE MIDDLE.

to keep you inside. It has a mattress, a toilet, and a sink.

A BIG question my kids asked was:
WHY DID YOU DO IT?

The short answer is, I wanted things
I didn't have the money for and I made
a bad choice in order to get them.

But really, I had what I needed.

And ultimately, my really bad choice took
away my ability to make choices on my own.

Sometimes when someone goes to prison, they think they are the only person impacted.

But there is so much more to it than that.

Families are left without someone they love and might feel ashamed, embarrassed, or sad.

Incarceration can impact a family's income, making it harder for them to pay for what they need.

In my case, the people who owned and worked for the places I robbed were impacted because I took things that were theirs in really scary ways.

My crime also impacted:

MY MOM.
MY DAD.
MY SIBLINGS.
MY COUSINS.
MY SCHOOL.
MY COMMUNITY.
AND MYSELF.

I let a lot of people down.

What I need you to know is...

INCARCERATION IM

PACTS EVERYONE.

Today, I reflect often on the people I hurt and the choices I made.

I know I can't take them back, but I can talk about it, listen, and be a part of helping others.

A big consequence of my choices was
being away from the people I love.

It was so hard to be away from my family, but thinking about them helped me get through each day.

My mom wrote to me

every

single

day

while I was in prison.

THAT'S
3,103
LETTERS!

She helped me not feel forgotten.

I knew when I looked at the sky
and saw the sun, the moon, and the stars,
my family was looking at the exact same sky
and it helped me feel connected to them...

even
though
I was
far away.

Some of you may be reading this book because you know someone who is incarcerated.

Some of you may want to know more about something that's happened to you or someone you love.

If that is you, I want you to know
that you can love someone and
not love the choices they've made.

You can also love someone
and not want them in your life.

Crimes are really bad choices.

And when someone we know and trust makes a bad choice it can be confusing.

And that's normal.

It's OK to need time to figure out your feelings.

But when you miss your person,
know that you can look up at the sky
and see the same one they are looking at.

I hope that brings you comfort like it did for me.

Some of you may be reading this book
because you are curious about incarceration
and want to learn more.

Despite what you know or may have heard, I'd like you to know the reason each person is in prison and their path to prison is different, and even the people who put them there make mistakes—it's not always fair.

I know people in prison who were wrongfully convicted, which means they didn't do the crime, but the judge believed they did.

I also know people who will be incarcerated for a very long time—maybe even the rest of their lives.

This makes me angry because sometimes the people who have the decision-making power get it wrong and don't always treat every person the same.

People have different
opinions about incarceration.

Some think it's a fair punishment, and others think there are better ways to make change and are speaking up about injustice.

I am here to tell you

CHANGE
AND GROWTH
ARE POSSIBLE
IN PEOPLE.

I am glad I never lost sight of this
and that I got a second chance.

My goals for the rest of my life
are to make safe and healthy choices
that actually bring positivity to myself,
my family and community, and
the world we all share.

Learning about the history of

INCARCERATION

will help us understand the long and ongoing work needed to make change in this country's legal systems.

I hope we keep learning and keep an open mind about people and know we can make a difference by asking questions and growing our understanding of incarceration.

Outro

Take a moment to check in with yourself and the kid you're reading with. How are you feeling? What do you need? What are you left wondering about?

Sometimes kids are ready for things grownups may not be ready for, and it's OK if your own feelings are different from your kid's. It's important to stay open-minded and be a supportive listener.

Continue to talk with kids about decision-making, consequences, boundaries, peer pressure, healthy relationships, conflict resolution, forgiveness, and healing so they build the tools to navigate life's ups and downs safely and effectively.

Want to go even deeper? Engage in conversations about the school-to-prison pipeline, mass incarceration, law and policy, and prison reform. Teach children to ask questions about the world around them and reflect on the person they want to be. Look to additional resources like counselors, social workers, and youth programs in your area.

Thank you for reading this book and getting the conversation started.

books about

confidence, imagination, anger, life online, addiction, grief, alzheimer's, optimism, gratitude, depression, and empathy.

a akidsco.com

Glossary of Terms

Crime: an act or acts done by a person that are against the law.

Incarceration: the act of putting someone in prison or jail, which restricts their rights.

Jail: a place people go when they have been accused of committing a crime and are awaiting trial or have been sentenced to serving a shorter amount of time.

Mandatory Minimum Sentencing: a fixed punishment for a crime, which does not take into consideration any circumstances around the crime.

Prison: a place where people who are convicted of a crime go after a court or judge decides their punishment.

Sentence: a punishment that spells out the length of time a person will be incarcerated, usually decided by a court or judge.

Victim: someone who is hurt or affected by a negative circumstance or another person's choices.

Words You May Also Hear With Incarceration

Inmate: a person who is incarcerated in jail or prison.

Mass Incarceration: how the United States has imprisoned a large population of people with an uneven and unfair focus on minority groups.

Maximum Security Custody: a prison that provides the highest level of security. Inmates are often surrounded by razor-wire fencing or walls and closely monitored by guards and cameras.

Penal System: anything that has to do with legal punishment. Prisons are a part of this system.

Racial Disparities: the unfair imbalance in treatment of different racial groups.

Restorative Justice: a process that views crime as more than breaking the law, recognizing the harm caused to people, relationships, and the community. The purpose of restorative justice is to repair harm and restore those damaged relationships.

Social Justice: the view that everyone's human rights deserve to be protected and that everyone should have equal opportunities.

State Penitentiary: A prison maintained by a state within the US.

notes

share
your read*

*Tell somebody, post a photo, or give this book away to share what you care about.

 **@akidsco**